A Book of Poetry and Prose

By

Craig Lynch

Published in the United States by Edit-Expert
Los Angeles, CA

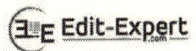

Edit-Expert

Cover Image: Annie Fourguette© (used with permission)
Cover Design: Edit-Expert

Copyright © 2018 Craig Lynch
Moments
A Book of Poetry and Prose

First Edition, August 2018

ISBN: 9781718129474

Table of Contents

In This Book	1
The Friend I Never Knew	2
Close Your Eyes	4
The Wonder Year	5
Hide and Seek	6
Trials of Faith	8
Grace	10
My Little Girl	11
Dad	12
Fighting Within	13
Protege	14
Psalm 4	17
Psalm 51	18
Psalm 2	19
Psalms 3	20
Psalms 1	21
Psalm 23	22
Never Alone	23
Time	26
Music From the Era	27
Jesus Freak	28
The Day	30
Joanne My Wife	31
Wondering	32
Our Love	33

I Am	34
My Love	35
Life Journal	36
Break It Off	37
The Reason for the Season	38
New Frontier	39
Psalm 56	40
The Pantomime	43
Psalm 53	44
Calendar Book	45
DAD	46
Many Roads	47
Learning to Cope	48
Cats	49
Death	50
Another Life is Gone	51
Mother's Day	52
Father's Day	53
A Moment of Happiness	54
Searching	55
Death of a Kamikaze	56
No Time	57
Hands	58
The Measure of Love	59
Leaves	60
Love	61

The Mistake	62
Birth Certificate	63
A Living Process	64
The Mug Shot	65
Her Day	66
Walls	68
Hidden Enemy	69
I'm Human	70
Undeserving	71
Alone Not with Christ	72
A Child of God	74
One Factor	75
Not A Gamble	76
Out of My Dreams	77
Death of a House	78
Life of a Home	78
Life-Threatening	79
There is an Answer	80
Wanting to Die	82
Touch of Beauty	83
A Toast	84
Lingering Love	85
Come Home	86
Joann (aka Joni)	87
Sparking Crustal Ray	88
Life Goes On	89

A Sad Love Song	90
Only Half Man	91
Majestic Love	92
River of Love	94
Lover and Wife	95
Love's Call	96
The Ones I Miss	97
Memory Halls	98
Sweet Potatoes	99
Who's Reality	101
Golden Days of Yore	102
Shadows	103
9 - 11 - 01	105
Eyes of Sorrow	106
Memories	107
Living Without You	109
A Mother's Lullaby	111
A Young Man's Treasure	112
Don't Point that at Me	114
Yesterday	115
A Simple Song	116
Springtime of Life	117
Place in the Corner	119
Ericka	120
Andrew	121
To Be Young Again	122

A Day at Work	123
A Child's Dreamland	124
The Working Man	125
The Family Tree	126
Crazy	127
Love You	128
Rose	129
Frogs	130
Lois (aka Angela Davis)	131
Christmas Memories	132
I Remember	134
Spilled Drinks	135
These are my Thoughts & Ideas	137
Darkness	137
Movement	138
Me	138
Life	139

In This Book

IN THIS BOOK
YOU SHALL FIND
ALL THE SECRET THOUGHTS
OF MY MIND

CONCEALED IN THESE PAGES
OF GOOD TIME GONE
MAY BE FOUND
MY UNWRITTEN SONG

THE LYRICS ARE SIMPLE
THE MEANING IS DEEP
READ VERY CAREFULLY
THE MEMORIES I REAP

WITHOUT ANY REASON
AND VERY POOR RHYMES
I'LL SHOW TO YOU
MY LIFE AND TIMES.

The Friend I Never Knew

Memories whispering in my ear
The times from so long ago,
All the days that use to be
The wonder years we all know

Minutes were quickly ticking by
Each hour seemed to run away
As minutes change to hours
The hours giving us a new day

All the yesterdays we use to have
All those days we left behind
So much for us to remember
Conjuring memories in our mind

Bits of life's moments stored away
All the friends we had back then
As well as those we didn't know
But we would see them again and again

Knowing them only by sight
As we went from day to day
Many years later crossing paths
But not knowing what to say

Catching up all the stories we had
Talking on and on for such a long time
Many things we have in common,
The many times our lives' did rhyme

We can only be long lost friends

For life has taken us in different directions
I wish we would have been friends
Back in the day we should have made a connection

The Lord has put us on different tracks
I wish I had known you, it's true
But those days are gone for good
You are, the friend I never knew

Close Your Eyes

I'm walking down the corridors
I feel so alone I could cry,
Loneliness consumes the darkness
There is no end to this feeling inside

There are many doors but where do they lead
Further emptiness is what I fear
I dare not venture into the rooms
I might see who I am in the mirror

If I look deep inside any room
I'm afraid of what I will find
What if it's hanging there on the wall
In the deep dark recesses of my mind

I know it is, so close the door
Don't let anyone else see my shame
This door, that door, or any door
For you see each room is the same

You will see where I have failed
Each room is filled with my pride
So close your eyes if you enter in
For in here is everything I am

The Wonder Year

All my years with puff, ahh so long ago
Those wonderful majestic days of yore
Slipping into and out of those times
During those years that we did explore

I look for you wherever I go
But you are nowhere to be found
I've looked in the waters of the deep
But you were nowhere around

It is said you can live forever
In those happy and playful times
I wish I could return to those days
When I could hear the music and rhymes

You once lived by the seashore
Or in the caves that line the way
You were there for the young of heart
And would never lead them astray

I loved to travel with you
On your boat we did sail
As I gave a look out for you
Anything that would prevail

I have sailed beyond those days
But there are others the same
And they will enjoy your dragon tales
Once you roar out your name

Hide and Seek

Let's play, tag you're it
I'll hide and you seek
He will never find me in here
He'll look but chances are bleak

I will have to be very quiet
So He will not hear me
But He might figure it out
For there is no guarantee

Well how did You find me
I was hiding really good
What, You always know
Wow, I didn't know You could

No, You can't know my thoughts
How then do you read my mind
I can see everything very well
You say I can't see, that I'm blind

But I can see the flowers in the field
As well as the birds in the air
You say I don't know Who You are
My knowledge has been impaired

I want to know Who You are
So please open my eyes
Ah, yes, I do see You now
I can see past all the lies

You have lifted my life beyond the stars
Now I see it is not a game
So I won't hide as I seek You out
For it is Your Son that I claimed

Trials of Faith

Oh no, look at what's ahead
I'm not sure what to do
We don't have any food or money
How will we make it through

I worry myself to death
Knowing it will do no good
But what else should I do
I guess praying is a likelihood

We have so many unpaid bills
And this just adds to the stress
If I bring it to the Lord
I'm afraid we won't be blessed

I have such little faith
Don't know if He will provide
Yes He feeds the birds of the air
But it's for me that He died

Yes He rose from the grave
For sin could not hold Him back
I've accepted Him as my Savior
But it's faith that I lack

He has been there many times before
And has blessed us beyond belief
It's my sinful self inside
That's what is giving me grief

So Lord I cry out for You to hear
Please refresh your Spirit in me
So it will increase my faith
For it is You, Who set me free

Grace

I hide from You
In all my guilt
Seeking to hide
From the sin I built

No matter where I go
You have been there before
I hide my face
It's you I try to ignore

I hide in deep dark places
Where no one has ever been
But here deep within my mind
I can't escape You or my sin

It's here where I find You
As we stand face to face
You put Your arms around me
And gently whisper, I offer my heart

My Little Girl

My little girl is gone
Grown and moved away
Many years since have passed
But I still remember the day

When Cinderella danced across the room
And straight into my heart
Wonderful were the times
Memories that never part

Times when at play
Gliding down the slide
Daddy close your eyes
You seek after I hide

I miss my little girl And the games we played
I miss my little girl Each and every day

My sweet little girl
She grew up so fast
The memories that I have
Are from the distant past

But as she goes on
In this world of dreams
She will find out for herself
What her life really is

Dad

I found an old box
I haven't seen in years
Afraid of what I will find
As I wiped away the tears

Inside this treasure of love
Letters of love from my wife
We will always be together
As we journey in this life

But there on the bottom
Were three little notes
I burst into tears
From letters my Dad wrote

I was surrounded with his memories
As I read each and every word
Traveling back to the time in his life
When all this did occur

I love him today as I did back then
Knowing his life was sealed
I know I will see him again
And he will be all healed

He was transferred from this life
To his life with the Lord
Now he is happy and healed
For God has given him his reward

Fighting Within

Many of the young kids
Go off to foreign lands
Not that they want to
But that was the command

Leaving the security of home
Off to a distant shore
Not knowing what to expect
As they go off to fight a war

First they must fight themselves
In order for them to kill
Many oppose this method
But others it gives a thrill

All of their days will turn dark
As light is gone from their eyes
Forcibly doing their part in war
And any values they must compromise

When they finally come home
And you look into those eyes
It's hard to see who they were before
For this person you do not recognize

Broken up in bits and pieces
So easily see with the eye
But many more wounds deep within
Hiding, not wanting to be identified

Protege

That which comes out
Is what is in the heart
From where does it come
Well, take a look at my chart

A reflection from the past
That which we let come in
All those who venture forth
Will be witness to all my sin

Over there behind that door
Are all the ones from yesterday
Yes, I hide them in there
Not wanting them on display

There are many other rooms
But please do not look inside
For in there my greatest sin
It's all do to my selfish pride

I live in my old sin nature
From when it first began
It slithered into our lives
Now it effects all of man

But Christ is part of my life
He dwells within my heart
He will always forgive us our sins
And He will never break us apart

Though each day builds upon itself
The Lord still loves us from day to day
We lift Him up and praise His name
For we alone are His protégé

Whispering

Echoing cries of loneliness
Whispering in the night
Solitude of the pre-dawn
Weary eyes declaring the light

Here I lie from the previous eve
A very brisk start of the day
Daily whining of what to come
It will happen no matter what you say

Rising with the lunar set
Wishing it never to go away
Loneliness departing from the night
Longing for that cabaret

The lonely still of the night
Reflecting that which had been
But it's peaceful in our solitude
For you see, I am my only friend

Peace and quiet is what we seek
In the orbit of who we are
Those who invade cross the line
And yes you leave a scar

Psalm 4

I call out to my righteous God
Please answer in my time of distress
I'm calling out for your relief
Have mercy on me as I'm being oppressed

How long will you fools seek false gods
As you continuously turn my glory to shame
The Lord has set His servants aside
He hears us when we call out His name

As you lay on your beds, quietly search your hearts
When you are trembling, do not sin
Offer the righteousness of your sacrifice
Trust in the Lord, for you know where you've been

The masses wonder who will bring freedom
Allow your light on us to shine
As their cups of wine and grain abounds
On this our joyful hearts will be divine

You offer a life full of peace
As I lie my head down to sleep
For Lord there is no one else
Who will dwell within their sheep

Psalm 51

Lord I cry out your name
Please have mercy on this my soul
Let your loving kindness dwell on me
As I give you my life and complete control

I have transgressed against you Lord
Please wash me from my sin
I ask for your merciful undying love
To cleanse my spirit deep within

In your presence I've performed acts of evil
I know as I travel about proclaiming you as mine
I sin against you and no one but you
In Your forgiveness I praise You divine

You bring me and others up on charges
I have been sinful since my birth
You rightly judge my actions in life
Lord, teach me your wisdom here on earth

Cleanse me with Your holy presence
Wash me so I will be whiter than snow
Lord, hide Yourself from my sinful past
Take my iniquities so they won't grow

Oh God, in Your majesty cleanse my heart
Pour out Your spirit unto me
As I seek the salvation You provide
Only in this shall I ever be free

Psalm 2

The nations do plan as the people plot
Kingdoms of the earth rise to the occasion
As rulers band with others the same
Against the Lord and His salvation

They claim tragedy against the Lord
As thunderous laughing consumes the land
The Lord, God rebukes them in His anger
And terrifies them that they cannot withstand

I will announce the Lord's decree
He spoke to me, you are my son
Today, forever, I am you Father
There is nothing else to be done

He will make all the nations my inheritance
And to the ends of the earth I will possess
With a rod of iron they will be broken
But It is I, that the Lord will bless

So you kings and rulers of the earth
You are to be wise as you are warned
Serve the Lord God, with fear and trembling
For if you do not, you will be scorned

Your road will lead to destruction
If you do not accept the right one
For His anger can flare in an instant
But blessed are they who choose His Son

Psalms 3

Lord there are many of those
Who rise up against me
Their demons are saying
You will not set me free

But my Lord God shields me
When I call out His name
He is the one lifting me up
His bellows from holy places came

He allows me to sleep
Though thousands are about
Standing guard till I wake
I will not fear there is no doubt

Arise and deliver me Lord
Break the jaws of my foe
Gather the wicked among them
Place them in the pit below

From you Lord comes deliverance
For all those You call sons
You bestow blessings upon us
For You say we are the ones

Psalms 1

If I do not walk in wicked steps
Or stand in the way that some take
Or sit in the company of those alike
Then I will be blessed in His name sake

But I will delight in Your law
And will study Your ways day and night
As my roots are planted in Your word
Bearing fruit due to Your power and might

Not so for those who come from the wicked
For they are like dust that blows away
So they will not stand in the Judgement
This is what the Lord does say

The Lord watches over His righteous
And will bring us into His presence
But those who rise with the wicked
Will receive death as unworthy peasants

Psalm 23

As I walk through this
The valley of the shadow of death
You say to me not to fear
But I fear at each and every breath

I know you are with me
So there is nothing that I lack
I'm allowed to lie in the pastures green
As You calm the waters and hold them back

You are the Shepherd of life
Providing comfort to your sheep
With Your rod and Your staff
But not those who still sleep

You guide me through this journey
You continually refresh my soul
I will always praise Your name
You Lord, are the one in control

You gather a table around me
Even in the presence of my foes
You sanctify me with oil
You bless me so, my cup overflows

I know that Your greatness and love
Will be with me to the end
I will forever live in Your House
A dwelling place without sin

Never Alone

I would like to say if I may
You are the one in my life
Who has always been at my side
So we became husband and wife

With all our times together
And the memories that we share
The Lord made us for each other
There is none other to compare

I loved you then as I do today
And when tomorrow is here
I will love you in the morrow
My love there is nothing to fear

When we are taken back
Kneeling down at His Throne
We will be together Eternally
By His side never alone

Life is Serene

I can see it all
Oh so deep inside
Viewed clearly throughout
In my mind's eye

But I can't lay it out
Before you or me
It's buried so deep
It's so hard to see

Thoughts that are buried
From many years gone by
When will I ever learn
Not to make you cry

I wish I could sing
It seems to soothe the soul
I would sing your tears away
Once again making you whole

But you have cried so often
In this life that we share
I just love you so much
As we continue this love affair

You're the most beautiful woman
I have ever known
Glancing into your eyes
That's where it is shown

The beauty of your spirit
In those shades of green
We will grow old together
Oh life is so serene

Time

How do we define an era
Is it running through an image
Which is buried deep within
As we go through the image
We are older looking back on your youth

That which we have done
Would it come out as before
Or would it change the way
The current of life goes

We wash up on the bank
Just to rest our weary souls
Rested, we climb back in
Dealing with life as we go

Should we go to the left
Or do we swerve to the right
Dealing with the present
While we are making our past

In our pursuit of this world
Memories that we reap
Clustering thoughts deep within
Staging memories that we keep

In the seasons of the past
Letting time go by
We are threading our stitches
In the fabric of time

Music From the Era

All the familiar songs
Keep ringing in my ears
Following the sound of each note
Drifting into younger years

Hurdles we have conquered
They lay in our past
Wisdom we have gained
From the trials that were cast

Peace we felt back then
Will always be there
As we go into tomorrow
We know we are prepared

That which takes us back
To the time we loved so well
A simple smile gives
Ah yes, I remember that carousel

Memories of our life
Rekindled from her kiss
Revealing life together
With my loving Princess

Memories that take us back
Those tunes we know so well
The music swirling within
This is where we dwell

Jesus Freak

In my youth
Back in the day
We made fun of you
Jesus Freak we would say

A friend and I would meet
Down at Manhattan Beach
We avoided you then
Not wanting to hear you preach

We would turn around
When you came our way
Not wanting to hear
What you had to say

Do you know Jesus
He loves you as you are
With all your blemishes
And all your scars

I pray I was what
You were back then
Living a life for God
Forgiven of your sins

Yes I know Jesus Christ
And I did back then
I was just bogged down
In my everyday sins

I thought I wasn't worthy
To call the Lord my own
But He forgives us of our sins
And never leaves us alone

The Day

The winter mist chills to the bone
As I sit here waiting for you
Please my love do not give up
Without you I will live in solitude

The lonely times will soon be here
I so long for our days in the past
As I hold you close to my side
Oh my love, I thought those days would last

The beauty that shows forth
Radiates from those shades of green
We thought our love would last forever
And we would not let anything intervene

I vowed myself to you alone
You have always been in my dreams
I long for those sensations once more
But something has blocked the streams

I picked these flowers with you in mind
I will place them with others on the ground
I could taste the fragrance in each one
As I laid them on your mound

Joanne My Wife

I saw you in a midsummer dream
Reaching out to touch the sky
I took you by your outstretched hand
But you didn't know the reason why

Warm winds bouncing off the stars
As the heavens above came alive
Overwhelmed with your presence
As memories of you were revived

Our hearts bound together as one
Increasing in strength each new day
With the love we have for one another
This is what I want to convey

I love you so much more than I did before
In this glorious life that we share
Looking forward to the years ahead
As we continue our love affair

Wondering

I look at you now
And I start to wonder
Wondering where you will be
At this point in my life

As though I'm looking in a mirror
And you're the one reflecting back
I've been there many times before
Tripping over life's hidden tracks

You're in that time of life
That I was back then
Struggling to survive
Struggling the trials again and again

These times they come and go
Seeming they are always there
They're here to make us stronger
As we go from year to year

There will be a time
When you will look back
You have worn those shoes
As you watch your own on life's track

Our Love

I'm lost in a dimension
In the back of my mind
Memories of you, my wife
Who I have enshrined

I have framed your picture
And placed it deep within my heart
This is where it will be
It will never ever depart

I think of you often
In this life that we share
The love that we have
Is definitely beyond compare

I love you today
More than I did back then
I will pour out my love
Only to you again and again

You are in my dreams
When I close my eyes
The memories that come forth
This is what satisfies

I don't want to wake up
Be if this is a dream
Our love for one another
Is always very extreme

I Am

The past is so easy to see
Well, I've been there before
But what does the future hold
Not knowing what is in store

I can't predict the future
Not knowing what lies ahead
Shall I follow my inward urges
Or should I follow You instead

Yes You are part of my life
As I go from day to day
There is the will of my flesh
But it's You I want to obey

The things I want to do
Are so hard to achieve
But that which I don't want
Is very easy to receive

Your Spirit dwells within
But my flesh is there too
I want to follow in Your path
But it is so hard to do

It is not I, that is dark inside
But that which is evil in the land
You sacrificed your One and only Son
From His resurrection He took command

My Love

We met on a Monday afternoon
Just down the street at the K-Mart
You slowly walked up to me
I stopped as you captured my heart

Then one day you went away
Consumed in darkness was I
Why did you leave so quickly
And you never said goodbye

The things we use to do
All the times that we shared
You were my one and only love
But I was totally unprepared

Memories of you in my life
Bouncing off the walls in our room
Emotions swirling around inside
And the smell of sweet perfume

The things that remind me of you
And all the games we would play
Going down to where we first met
Oh, my eyes begin to give away

I'm not sure I can love again
I wish we could talk, have a dialogue
Oh Sadie you can never be replaced
Never will I find such loyalty in a dog

Life Journal

Memories bouncing off each page
As I read an old journal I found
Engulfing in the visionary past
Memories of old that are so profound

Years come forth from younger times
Exposing an era we know so well
Those days in which we struggled
The experiences that we can retell

I have been there once before
So be careful as you go about
Learn the ups and downs life will give
As you go there is no doubt

As you go, reflect the knowledge
That you have learned in life
Others might escape life's hardships
As they experience less strife

Break It Off

Well here we are once again
We have been here many times before
But now I want you to leave
And quit knocking on my door

Yes, at one point we held hands
But that was so long ago in the past
I tried over and over to break it up
I don't want this relationship to last

I dare not let you in
Please depart from me
Your opinion differs from mine
There is no way we'll agree

The influence that you had on me
Yes, it was something I did believe
I wanted you in my life back then
But now I want you to leave

I found someone else to love
So our relationship will not be restored
I want nothing to do with you anymore
For I have given my life to the Lord

The Reason for the Season

The seasons they come and they go
But this time of year should stay
We all dance about in joyous times
But it's more than just a holiday

For on this day a child was born
He was born for me and for you
A lot of folks refuse to believe
But I will tell you, it is true

It is true that God loves us for who we are
Not that which you think you must be
He lived on earth and died for us
In doing so, He set us all free

We come together as a nation
To celebrate His birth every year
For those who really know Him
There is absolutely nothing to fear

We allow Him to rule in our lives
For He is our Savior, Jesus Christ
He loves everyone to come to Him
And accept Him as their sacrifice

New Frontier

Watching as you go through your life
A collection of memories throughout the years
From childhood up to the present day
Out of all that time, a new life premieres

It's sad to live those early years
All the carefree moments that were explored
Must move on as new adventures come forth
Realizing the early days will not be restored

But they will be safely planted
As souvenirs deep within the mind
For that's where our treasures are stored
And that's where they will be enshrined

Each item carries different memories
Reminiscent, a generation in the past
Not knowing what the future will hold
Not knowing the memories that will be cast

While traveling in this, the parade of life
A collection of memories from year to year
There are many that are cast aside
Others giving wisdom for the new frontier

Psalm 56

Oh my God, please shower me with compassion
My adversaries are striving against me
Each day they seek me with harm
Only in You do I have my guarantee

They rival against me all day long
We seek to destroy you, they cried
Searching for me with weapons at hand
Their strongest weapon being their pride

My trust in You never does it waiver
Praising You though frozen in fear
With You and Your everlasting word
No one can touch me or interfere

They distort the meaning of my words
They wish my life to go away
Lord please do not let them escape
Destroy those in their wickedness today

Oh Lord God, please register my grief
Wipe away my tears in Your scroll
They will turn about as I call for You
For they will see, You are in control

Then, again,

Lord God I praise You and Your word
For what can a nation of man do to me
I trust in You and will never fear
I seek You out on bended knee

I vow to You as I give my offerings
You stopped me from stumbling like mere men
Allowing me deliverance from death
So I may walk with our King again and again

Solitude

In the slumber of the eve
The dream center of life
Carried off to a different place
That land without any strife

The happenings of yesteryear
Silhouetted so deep within
The doubts of tomorrow
Not knowing where to begin

This is where fairytales are found
To escape the realities to come
Dancing to a different beat
Not that of our own drum

In here no tears are shed
Though droplets of loneliness do abound
Come in but watch your step
Or this is where you'll be found

There you are sitting alone
No escape from your solitude
Others have offered to help
But you don't like the attitude

Seems as though I've been here before
So many times it did occur
For some it's hard to get out
But for me, I am not an amateur

The Pantomime

Looking at my tomorrows
Yesterday has already been
Today I stand in the present
But I still hear that violin

It sings so softly
The melodies of life
When it plays out of tune
It cuts as deep as a knife

That which we have done
Mistakes we have made
Walking from day to day
Playing this game of charade

Dancing in the moments of life
Listening to its music as we go
Not wanting to lose its rhythm
So we take it nice and slow

Walking to our own beat
As we live our life and time
Going as steady as we can
Watching each step in this pantomime

Psalm 53

The fools say there is no God to bow down to
In all ways they are corrupt and vile
So says the ignorant fool in his heart
They strangle on foolishness and drown in their bile

Mankind is seen from far above
The Lord looking for any, who understand
But there is no one who seems to stand out
These evildoers cannot see what God planned

Those who practice their own ways know nothing
They chew up my followers and spit them out
They appear to be overwhelmed in fear
They would not have fear if they didn't doubt

The Lord scattered the remains of those
The ones who harmed God's select
They were put to shame and despised by God
When you don't love God this is the effect

Israel seek out your salvation
From Zion let it come to you
Jacob and Israel will rejoice in gladness
Let God restore His people anew

Calendar Book

I found a calendar the other day
Many years have since past
Several days in each month
I saw what was cast

Written in those days gone by
Oh yes, so many years ago
Appointments that were made
Things she had to know

Going from one day into the next
Her schedule was well in place
Days and places in the future
All that she had to embrace

It belonged to my Mother-in-law
This tablet I held in my hands
Different days in different weeks
There was everything she had planned

But then in this calendar book
There was nothing beyond September
That's when we lost her
Those days I will always remember

DAD

Yes he walked on water
At least that's how it seemed
I watch him many times
In the sleeplessness of my dreams

As I lay awake each night
His life echoes in my mind
Silhouetted in this heart of mine
And all the memories you will find

Though life's waters run deep
And waves crashed upon his feet
He never wavered from his task
He would never seek a retreat

There was so much he would do
Without even batting an eye
As I look back on it now
It's hard not to cry

I miss him so much every day
Knowing this is how it must be
I know I will see him again
In the presence of God in eternity

Many Roads

There are many roads to follow
As we travel down this road of life
Stay close and do not waver
So you won't fall into the pit of strife

As I walk from this day into the next
The wonders that I will find
Venturing into the hall of memories
Into the deep dark recesses of the mind

The times that were
Will they ever be the same
If we could do it all over
Would that time still be found

Or could we venture forth
Beyond the boundaries that were laid
Traveling down a different road
Creating a much different parade

If we march to a different drummer
Would all the memories be the same
Or would it change the person within
And all that we became

Once it has come and gone
We can't change the past
The person who lives within
Is that which was cast

Learning to Cope

Sitting in my shell
Unbroken to the world
Living the reality
Of my covering

Unhatched to competition
Years slip by
Nested and sat upon
By the warmth of knowledge

Overnight
My shell is cracked
Piece by piece
Being chipped away

Now
Revealed to the world
No more protection
No riding authority
On my own

Fighting
Struggling
Winning
Losing
But learning

Learning to cope
In this changing world

Cats

Cats are sly and tricky
Slowly sneaking up to their prey
Stocking it with determination
Watchfully planning an attack

Each move is precise
Waiting for the correct time
When his prey is unalert

Then in a split second
He jumps
Capturing it unexpectantly

My love is like a cat
Sneaky
Sly
Unpredictable
Moving at the right time
Patiently waiting

Then when you least expect it
I'll lunge
Capturing your heart

Death

Lying in bed
Thick dark clouds roll into sight
Darkening my dreams forever
Crying louder and louder
No one hears my pleas for help

Silence falls
Adrenaline flows
Pounding heartbeat
Rapid Breathing
But yet everything is silent

Is anyone there
Reaching out
Feeling nothing
Fall to the floor
But feel nothing

Crying again and again
Can anyone hear me
I cannot
Lying in a dead trance
Moist salty lips
Smell of formaldehyde
Fills the room

Never before have I appreciated
Life so much
Until it was gone

Another Life is Gone

Running down the beach toward the water
Bombs bursting in the air
Bullets flaring in all directions
The sergeant falls
Another life is gone

Reaching the water we run faster
Waves crash against our legs
Bullets rip into my buddies back
My buddy falls
Another life is gone

Swimming hard and fast to reach the ship
Blood all over the water
Sharks swimming around in circles
Pete goes under
Another life is gone

Climbing on board ship safe on deck
Zeroes zipping through the air
Shooting their metal fireflies towards us
I fall down hard
Another life is gone

Mother's Day

Mother's Day only comes once a year
And to many women
Brings a smile and a tear
The smile comes from
The warm love shared
And the tears come from
Every woman's fear

The fear of thinking
That in a year or two
Your children will grow up
And forget all about you
But remember these words
No matter how grown up I seem
You will always be in my dreams

Father's Day

Fathers have a special day too
It's a day set aside just for you
A day of peace and rest
When every child is at his best

On this day they will hold you high
For all the world to see as you pass by
Your children will beam with pride
As the world sees you through their eyes

For you see
Your children love you a lot
And this is a price
Which cannot be bought

A Moment of Happiness

For a moment in time
I held you

Then
Like the passing of the night
It was over

The time we shared
Was that of a dream

You were mine
And I was yours

It was like a fairy tale
As in all fairy tales

It was in the realm of fantasy
A fantasy with no end in sight
Until reality resumed its proper identity

Searching

If I searched the world over
In the distant lands
In every valley
On every mountaintop
I would never find another person
As lovely as the one I found in you

Death of a Kamikaze

For no apparent reason
The kamikaze dives towards the water
Followed by another
He pulls out of it
Leaving a wake of courage

His young follower soars with determination
He pulls too late
And plunged into the murky darkness
He struggles with frustration
Seeking an escape

His friends flock above with concern
Unable to do a thing
His snow crest wings darken
In the dingy liquid

He gives cries of help without assistance
Twisting and turning
But only sinks further

He goes under
The oily sea
Takes another gull

No Time

People coming and going
No place to go
Seeming never to stay home

Girls scurry about
Waiting
Taking orders

Night after night
Same people
Same orders
Same old routine

Girls running
Trying to keep up with people
Cooks throwing out orders
Cashiers ringing up totals

No one stays home anymore
Always moving
Always in a hurry
No spare time
No time for theirs

This is no life
But it's the one we made
And the one we have to live

Hands

Your hands
Always hide
Your face

Move your hands
For a minute
So I can see

I watch you
Day in
And day out

But still
Do not know
The proper time

Can you move
Your hands
So I can see

After all
You have
The time

The Measure of Love

Who dares to
measure my love for thee
A man of fools
Or a man of riches

If so
How long be his ruler

No product of man
Can measure our love
Only we can measure
Our love for one another

Tell me
How do I
Measure to thee

Leaves

Leaves depart with the wind
Swirled about
No home
No destiny
No roots
Belonging to nobody but themselves

I'm different
I want a home
A destiny
I want us to be one
Belonging to nobody
But each other

I don't want to be a leaf
Relying only on the wind
I want to be a man
Relying on our love

Love

Love is a word
Which is indescribable

And you're a person
With the same character

The Mistake

People come and go
Frantically smoking
Saying goodbye

The room heavily guarded
Making sure no one gets out of line
Uniformed men scurry about

Inside
They're offered a last smoke
Wheeled down a long pathway

Strapped in
Tensed bodies
Looking to heaven
Seeming to say
Please God give me another chance

But it's too late
They already bought their one-way ticket
All that needs to be done
Is to flip the switch

Each prisoner tightly strapped in
Muttering silent prayers
At the proper time
The switch is flipped
The engines fire up
And the big jumbo jet
Taxi's down the runway

Birth Certificate

A documentation of life
Why do I have to be documented
To prove that I'm alive

Look you fool
Just open your eyes
Read my certificate
Craig Lynch
ALIVE

A Living Process

The disease is contagious
Coming without warning
Showing no partiality
Taking both young and old
Rich and poor

Some are prepared
Waiting for it to come
And taking it
For what it really is
Others fear it
And dread the thought
It can happen to them

Some take precautions
Others just wait
Someday we'll have to
Look it straight in the face
And accept Death for what it is
A Living Process

The Mug Shot

Among the lineup
Wondering why
Why he's in here

Grubby beard
Stringy mustache
Long curly hair
A typical hippie

Glaring blue eyes
Rough looking face
Grimy clothes
A portrait of an ex-con

A snarl
Replaces a smile
Yellowed teeth
Pale face
An expression of sorrow

Appears to be a mug shot
But it's not
It's my driver's license

Her Day

The day is finally here
Mother is all teary eyed
And father doesn't say a word
This is the day for their baby
The one who grew up so fast

Friends and relatives
Have come many miles for this day
There is Aunt Sue
Whom she hadn't seen in years
One of her best friends
Who moved away last summer
And an old boyfriend
How nice that he came
Look
Even a tear
Showing he has no hard feelings

The room
Beautifully decorated with flowers
Candles lit behind the preacher
And soft organ music
Setting the mood

As she is escorted down the aisle
Still others break into tears
People gasp
At the surprising beauty
Radiating from her face
An expression of accomplishment
That she finally made it

She gets the ministers blessing
Then he says a long prayer
Emphasizing the seriousness
And that it only happens once in life

Then everyone scurries outside
To see one last time
Before they
Lower her in the ground

Walls

Walls
All around me
A new day
A new wall
Blocking my view
Blocking the real me
Wherever I go
I find another wall

I'm unknown
Unknown to the world
And unknown to myself
I'm looking
Searching for the real me
Hoping
Wondering
Which wall I'm behind

Hidden Enemy

The cry echoes
Throughout the land

You take up arms
Battle stations are posted
Communications are opened
Defense tactics are analyzed

You wonder
Which way will they attack
By land
By air
Or by sea

But your enemy is hidden
He attacks your soul

I'm Human

Look at me
Take a good look
What am I
Who am I

I'm me
I'm not a great prophet
Scholar
Or even very intelligent

I'm just like you
I have emotions
I cry
Laugh
And even get mad

I have the same
Desires you have
Look at me
I'm human too

Undeserving

He taught
Did we listen

He healed people
Did we believe

He suffered
Did we understand

He resisted
Did we

He offered all
Do we deserve it

Alone Not with Christ

Alone am I
Alone I stand
Alone I fall
And alone I lay

The world passes by
No one stops
No one looks
And no one cares
People walk by
They push and shove
Push me when I get up
And kick me when I'm down
Walk right over me
Plow right through me
Not caring about my feelings

Then someone cared
Smiling
Our hands came together as one
I grasped it as tight as I could
Fearing to let go

He pulled me off the ground
Pulled me out of my pain
Sorrow
And self-pity
Pulled me out of my grief
And up to His love

Now I try
To hold firm to that hand
Sure I fall
But He is always there
There to pick me up again

A Child of God

Coming into the world
New
Fresh
Sinless

Heir to a fortune
Inheriting all
Staying in this prestige
As long as he's a child of God

One Factor

Child
Teenager
Or adult
Age has no limit

White
Black
Red
Or Yellow
It makes no difference

Broke
Unemployed
Poor
Rich
Or in between
Wealth is not needed
But Christ is

Not A Gamble

The fisherman patiently waits
For the big one

The bookie anxiously waits
For the results

Race drivers speed
For the checkered flag

The stockholder carefully
Plays the market

And the Christian awaits His return
But it's not a gamble

Out of My Dreams

You came from my dreams
And into my life
My companion
By my side

Not under my feet
Or over my head
But be my side
To share my joys
And hardships

Together we share love
And with God's greatness
We can create human life
Circling around Him
We will have perfect love
Forever

Death of a House
Life of a Home

Silence falls on the household
Someone has left
No more does he live here

Taking the Home
Leaving only the House
The abandoned house
Will never be occupied again

He left his house
But yet
Is a very rich man

Yes he died
And left his house
But his home
He took with him

Life-Threatening

Every day
It threatens their lives
Some unaware
But yet
They walk with death
Wondering
Hoping it isn't true
We know it's true
But we don't walk with fear
We're aware
It's not threatening
We know
We won't die
But live once again
Forever

There is an Answer

People are a big let down
You look up to them
They show you the way
You think they're great
You think they're religious
Without having too many faults
You're floating along on a high
You feel close to your Creator

Then this friend falls away
You no longer look up to him as before
Instead you fall away too
You lose that high you were riding on
You lose that closeness to your Creator
And lose faith in all you do
You feel like dropping everything
Getting away from it all right now
You're trying to find yourself
And where you're going

You finally find it
It's not looking up to your friends
Expecting them to show you the way
It's not being on a man-made high
Instead it's looking up to Jesus Christ
Looking up to Him to show you the way
His way for you

Going all out for Him
Giving your all in all
Being on a Godly high and much more
This is what it's all about

But the bummer is
It's hard and it's rough
Your friends will let you down
And disappoint you

But instead
Try to look to Christ
Because that's where it's at

Wanting to Die

Wanting to die
But for what
Something you believe in
Yes
A God you have never seen
Yes
A man you have only heard about
Yes
This and much more

Don't be anxious
Live it while you can
But live it for the Lord
Fighting for the cause
Adding to His Kingdom
Leaving assured
Knowing you have shown the way
For your family
Friends
Even your enemy

Remember someday
Your time will come
Then
I'll accept it
Yes
Grieving for your company
But joyous
For your Life

Touch of Beauty

The touch of your love
The smile in your eyes
Your tears of joy
Things that make you cry

The laughter in your voice
The love in your heart
A woman of beauty
A fine work of art

The sound of your voice
Sweet music to my ears
A melody of love
For all to hear

Golden brown locks
Shades of green in your eyes
Skin soft as silk
A woman without disguise

The beauty of your spirit
The climax in my life
This is what you brought
When you became my wife

A Toast

I raise my glass
And offer a toast
To a woman of beauty
Of whom I boast

To my love
Woman of my life
Who a year ago
Became my wife

Time has passed
My love lingers on
Each passing day
Brings a new song

A melody so sweet
That when it's heard
The meaning rings true
Each and every word

I sing it to you
As the years go by
I'll love you forever
Till the day I die

Lingering Love

To my beloved wife
Who I love the most
You're the wine I drink
As I make this toast

To the years gone by
To the things we've done
Our life together
And here's to our sons

The taste of your wine
So sweet on my lips
And I think of you
With each and every sip

I think of what I have
With you as my wife
When a year a go
You came into my life

This toast lingers on
It is always here
I love no other
There is nothing to fear

Come Home

When you are gone
Who will continue
To write the songs

The melody will disappear
Lost in the many miles
Drowned in my tears

The beat will be out of time
It will lose its rhythm
And have no rhyme

But my love will wait
Until you return
On that very special date

When you come home
I'll write a new verse
One that's true
One I won't need to rehearse

Joann (aka Joni)

I knew a girl named Joan
Who was constantly on the phone
When asked who she called
She would run down the hall
To scream and shout
What it was all about
She tells her story
It was all hunky-dory
But only she knew the truth
And would give her eye tooth
To talk on the phone
But that's just Joan

Sparking Crustal Ray

In the misty blue
Across the bay
You were captured for a moment
In the sparkling crystal ray

Gleaming pearls of white
Strung throughout your hair
Glistening color of green
In your eyes so fair

On a bridge of gold
With water at your feet
Waiting for your lover
Who you came to meet

Clouds of darkness
Cast shadows in my mind
Am I the one you wait for
Am I the one you'll find

A clanging symbol
Brings light to my eyes
The misty blue subsides
Causing the scene to die

I lay in sorrow
Wishing time to go away
So I can watch you again
In the sparkling crystal ray

Life Goes On

With the love God gave
We have our sons
Years of pleasure
Years of fun

Through the years
We'll watch them grow
Raising them in love
Teaching all we know

Growing to maturity
Seeking out their lives
They will marry
Taking their own wives

When that time comes
We'll let them go
Living their own lives'
As we did

A Sad Love Song

Another day passed
My love lingers on
Whistling the tune
A sad love song

It tells of a man
Very much deprived
Longing to be near
His long-awaited bride

The story's the same
A thousand times been told
Two lovers apart
Waiting for time to unfold

It's hard to be in love
When you're miles apart
The distance is a barrier
For two young hearts

Their passions build
As the years drag on
Whistling that tune
A sad love song

Only Half Man

I sit alone
Thinking about you
The crickets echo
My cries of loneliness

The night light
Signifies my life
Without you

The moon radiates
But half its face
The stars shine
Only half their strength

My life goes on
Without you
Only half a man......

Majestic Love

Once in a dream
It came to me
Do dreams come true
I'll wait to see

In slumber night
I had a vision
One of beauty
Our love had risen

Rising to new heights
Reaching its peak
One I must climb
For the beauty I seek

A treasure of worth
More valuable than gold
Listen to my story
As it is told

As prince charming
Searched for his beauty
As in the fairy tale
For that was his duty

He wasn't reality
But this is true
I'll seek out my beauty
Until I find you

And when you're found
The birds will sing
You'll be my bride,
symbolic of a ring

You'll be crowned
Queen of my life
You'll live in majesty
Ruling as my wife

River of Love

My love for you
Is ever growing
Just as a river
Continuously flowing

Each passing day
The waves increase
Gaining strength
It will never cease

Overflowing
The banks of love
Soaring high
As a flying dove

A river of peace
In a stormy sea
The love you give
Sets me free

Lover and Wife

I've said it before
Let me say it again
You're my wife, my lover
And my best friend

Being my wife
I have no need for more
You're the one I love
You're the one I adore

Our nights of solitude
With intimates embrace
Fulfills you as a lover
No other will I chase

We'll be best friends
Throughout our life
You'll be my lover
And you'll be my wife

Love's Call

Once in a dream
It came to me
Do dreams come true
Read on and you'll see

In the peace of slumber
It came to mind
you're the one I looked for
You're the one I'll find

I was asleep
During that time
But my eyes were opened
When you became mine

A dream I had
Of love's adore
You give me this
And very much more

You gave your life
The beauty of it all
To live with me
The answer to Love's call

The Ones I Miss

From the time we first met
To the embrace of our last kiss
Until the end of each day
You are the one I miss

I miss your caressing touch
Your heart pounding on my chest
I miss holding you close
While in my arms you rest

Probing the warmth of your soul
As we rest in love's embrace
Experiencing the depth of your being
I so long for this taste

At the end of each long day
Knowing we will share a kiss
This is what I long for
You are the one I miss

Memory Halls

Please close the door
And turn out the light
This is my hiding place
To avoid the fight

It's peaceful here
Deep in my mind
Retreating from battle
Of words unkind

Repressed memories hiding here
Each room securely locked
No keys to be found
For feelings I've blocked

Down the hall of memories
Some empty rooms you'll find
These rooms filling up later
With future events unkind

Sweet Potatoes

No – I don't like sweet potatoes
And It doesn't matter when
A Thanksgiving celebration
Or Christmas with our kin

When you pass it my way
I'll look at you with a smile
I do not like my potatoes sweet
It is just not my style

Don't say you make it different
And it tastes better than most
I don't want to offend you
After all you are the host

I've tried it many times before
And insulted many in the past
Sometimes they become angry
And I have to get out fast

Most times they are gracious
And overlook me being rude
I say I don't like sweet potatoes
And it's not a matter of ingratitude

At times my wife forces me
To try this dish I detest
Reluctantly I open my mouth
As she makes this request

I do my best not to gag
As this poison touches my lips
Should I tell her the truth
Hey – this isn't bad I quip

Who's Reality

As the nights turn into days
Such is the passing of time
Seasons watching the children grow
Waiting out the sounds of chimes

Unhatched to the realities of life
Nestled in the security of family ties
Longing to stretch beyond their boundaries
Waiting for the opportunity to try

I've been in their shoes before
Walking that path in my youth
Seeking to be out on my own
Seeking to learn reality's truth

Passing from our hands into their own
Apparently not caring for those left behind
Or for the grieving loss I feel
They seem undeterred and totally blind

Life will never be the same again
As life shatters before my eyes
Not grasping the heartbreak inside
Not hearing my private silent cries

This unsettling reality of life
Never did I expect to arrive
The exodus of children from home
The joy of their lives' I'll be deprived

Golden Days of Yore

Perched on the window sill
In the corner of my mind
People scurry to and fro
This place called mankind

Racing to make ends meet
Not stopping to say hello
Too busy for friendships
Neighbors you never know

In seasons from the past
Streets with nicely trimmed lawns
Society held values of God
But those golden days are gone

Gone to the wayside
Those virtuous days of yore
Revealed to the youth of today
They perceive to be folklore

Longing for the return of ethics
Those values from yesteryear
Waiting for the tide to turn
Waiting for people to be sincere

Shadows

Come follow me
See what you find
As we travel down
Memory halls of my mind

I'll show to you
My days of yore
Down this hallway
There are many doors

Behind each door
Mysteries of past
No light is shed
But shadows are cast

Some rooms are open
Others securely locked
Before entering in
Don't forget to knock

A boy in the corner
He sits over there
Timid and scared
LIFE
Is what he fears

Shadows of doubt
A world unknown
Rise to the occasion
Though all alone

The room next door
Is where I cry
Realities of life
Is where dreams die

9 - 11 - 01

The tears of our nation
Have flooded the land
Once dry and desolate
As the grains of sand

Now the waters flow free
And the hatred grows
The dam has been broken
Due to this barbaric blow

Our spirits have been wounded
Our nation is in distress
As our Lady of Liberty
Is put to the test

The healing process is slow
As the nation looks to God
We sound the trumpet to battle
Our foes have declared a jihad

We will fight in our cities
We will fight for our land
We will sift out our enemy
Through every grain of sand

Eyes of Sorrow

The sorrow you have
Is seen in your eyes
The Lord will comfort you
During your silent cries

He will lift you up
When you're feeling down
For the one you love
Received the Holy Crown

As waves of emotions
Rise in your heart
Gentle sweet memories
These.......will never part

As time goes by
This promise He makes
The ones He loves
Are the ones He takes

Memories

I was caught up in the past
With the scent of your perfume
Your presence filled my heart
As memories filled the room

Whisked off to a different time
Gazing into those shades of green
A time from our distant past
A time that was so serene

Memories of caressing moments
As we walked hand in hand
Strolling along the water's edge
Sailing into our own wonderland

Under a starlit night
Holding you close by my side
Dreaming of our life together
Dreaming of my future bride

Memories of driving in my truck
Following a road to its end
Oldies blaring from the radio
Our faces blasted by the wind

Love letters spanning the miles
Filling the void of lonely hearts
Letters of love rekindle the spark
While two lovers were apart

These memories of old
Of the life we share
There are many more to come
As we continue this love affair

Living Without You

Living without you in my life
Would not be worth living at all
Like water cascading down the mountains
Without the beauty of a waterfall

Just as God has brought rain upon the land
To bring nourishment and life to the earth
In the same way you have given to me
Without you my life would have no worth

Hard times come and hard times go
We've had our share of fights too
But after the dust has settled
Still I cannot live without you

At times you can make me angry
And the same for me I know is true
Even though our tempers will flare
I still do not want to live without you

There are many things I can live without
Such as the pain this life can bring
Or the morning birds perched in a tree
As they whistle the songs that they sing

Crickets serenading the departure of the sun
With echoing cries from frogs and toads
These wonders of nature I can live without
Even the sight of stars as they explode

In the morn when it rises in the East
Casting a rainbow of colors in the sky
Even this is something I can live without
No matter how pleasing it is to the eye

There are many things I can live without
As I go from day to day in this life
And with all the things I can go without
I can't live without you—my wife

A Mother's Lullaby

Is it happiness in her eyes that I see
As she slowly thumbs through the book
Viewing each picture from the distant past
Stopping to take a good long look

Do you want to see my favorite time
Looking up – with a tear in her eye
Pointing out when the kids were small
Remember this – she says with a sigh

Leaning over she kissed each likeness
Of those tiny faces from years before
Those children who have grown so quickly
These grown children that she so adores

A mother's grief comes straight from the heart
This sorrow that I see deep in her eyes
Flows from the loss of those times long ago
When she sang them those sweet lullabies

Melodies of night time serenades
Something that lingers in her heart
Captured forever in pictured memories
A mother's love that will never part

A Young Man's Treasure

When I was a young man
I stumbled across a trickling brook
Intrigued by its current beauty
I went for a better look

What I spied peaked my interest
Asleep in its home on the bed
A stone with an alluring glow
Take this treasure home a voice said

So I snatched it from its stream of slumber
To treasure and put it on display
I placed it on a shelf in my heart
That's where its beauty would stay

Others looked and stared at its brilliance
At the mystery of this stone of mine
Which I have treasured and locked in my heart
Where I put it on a shelf and made a shrine

Many years since have passed
From the shelf that pebble slipped away
Its appearance was tarnished and lost
It fell from where I had it on display

It fell to the floor with a loud crash
This stone that I treasured in my youth
It wasn't until that very moment
That it was revealed to me – the truth

I stared in disbelief and unimaginable regret
Before my eyes, my stone was broken
Take this treasure home and cherish it
Remembering as a young man those words spoken

It's luster gone appearing weathered and worn
Though years of neglect had taken its toll
I noticed something I hadn't seen before
From the broken stone a familiar glow

Still tarnished and in many pieces
Something reminded me of the days of old
This treasure I valued so in my youth
I now find is filled with gold

How could I have been so blind
How could I have been such a fool
The treasure I found in my youth
Wasn't an ordinary stone but a jewel

Now that I see the true value and worth
Is it possible to piece it together once more
If I could turn back the clock in time
Returning to my treasure as it was before

I want this precious jewel to be whole again
I want it to be restored in my life
To place it back on the shelf of my heart
For you see........
This stone I found in my youth
Is my wife

Don't Point that at Me

Don't point that thing at me
What would happen if it's loaded
What would you do if it misfired
Or worst yet if it imploded

Didn't your mama ever tell you
If you play with fire you'll get burned
Or were you just born stupid
It's something you never learned

Put it away before you hurt someone
I don't want that someone to be me
Put it down I'm warning you
I'll give you till the count of three

This is the last time I'll say it
Before I call in the swat team
Drop it and put your hands up
Or you're really going to get reamed

Don't point that thing at me
You don't know where it's been
Don't point your finger at me
I thought we were friends

Yesterday

All my yesterdays are gone
Silhouetted in my mind
All my tomorrows yet to come
Shadows I've yet to find

Yesterday I was dreaming in wonderland
Dancing and playing when I was young
Coloring books and nursery rhymes
And all the songs that I sung

A time wishing to last forever
Of heartfelt memories
Climbing up snow-capped mountains
The joy of a downhill ski

Each day marches into the next
Going from yesterday into tomorrow
The only thing certain is uncertainty
Will tomorrow bring joy or sorrow

Questions and answers of what lies ahead
Can't be questioned or answered at the time
Only when we take time to look back
We see our life – every rhythm and rhyme

We can't predict events of the future
Only decipher the choices we made
Learning from mistakes we encounter
As we continue on in this life crusade

A Simple Song

What is it about the past
Of all those good times gone
Buried so deep in the heart
But surfaces from a simple song

Melodies from a youthful era
In those enchanted days of yore
Soothing to our restless spirit
As we travel down that corridor

Hallways of sweet remembrance
Bring comfort in unsettling times
A decade of reminiscent music
Listening to those familiar chimes

Listening to those simple songs
Allowing us to escape from life
In those melodies from yesteryear
Will be found no worries or strife

Springtime of Life

Life was much simpler in those days of yore
I long for the carefree days of younger years
Gliding on the impromptu whim of youth
In an era that was so cavalier

Longing to lay once again on the neighbor's lawn
Sailing across crystal blue skies in my mind
To gaze at the scattered pillowed clouds
With youthful imagination wondering what I would find

More than mere ink blots in the summer sky
Seasoned winds chattering through the trees
Dancing leaves blow weightless to the ground
Joining their friends in cluster camps of refugees

Whatever happened to those days of happiness
When I could ride the fire and not get burned
When I could walk across the clouds and not fall
I could sail with the wind as the world turned

Journeys I followed were etched in my mind
Navigating the hopes and dreams of uncharted land
Just as the currents in the ocean of life
Tossing and turning the dreams that were planned

As sure as the clouds have darkened my days
Those wondrous times from long ago past
Were merely a moment during a season in time
I see now they were meant to last

In that time in the spring days of my life
I long for the carefree years when I was young
When life was simpler in those days of yore
In an era when a happier tune was sung

Place in the Corner

He sat in the corner
A frown on his face
Why did I get punished
Daddy – I hate this place

I held back the tears
When I looked in his eyes
You may not understand now
But we don't tell lies

He bit his lip
As he turned away
How long do I sit here
When can I go play

When I know you're sorry
And you see you were wrong
For you see these are the things
That will make a man strong

Even though I punish you
I don't want you to forget
I will never stop loving you
My love will never quit

From his place in the corner
He looked up after a while
Slowly that face with a frown
Turned into a loving smile

Ericka

There was a time
When she was small
A time of dress up
And playing with dolls

There was a time
I remember it well
She waved her wand
I was under her spell

There was a time
Not meant to last
Childhood memories
A little girl's past

I remember a time
The things she said
I remember a time
Every tear she shed

I remember a time
Seems so far away
I remember a time
It was yesterday

Andrew

With a slap of the hand
Could be heard the baby's cry
In no time at all
His first word, bye-bye

With the urging of the hand
He crawls to your side
When he takes his first step
A parent beams with pride

On his first day of school
He held me by the hand
I told him it would be okay
Just do as we had planned

He climbed in the front seat
Keep both hands on the wheel
When can I drive solo Dad
As soon as you get the feel

Today he will graduate
His life he will start to plan
On his own hard work ahead
But you see – today he is a man

To Be Young Again

Ah to be young again
To do as I never did
To go around once again
Capturing that moment as a kid

To be young again
Would I do the same
Would I make mistakes alike
Still being the one to blame

Would I still be at fault
For decisions that I make
Suffering from ill choices
This is what I'm afraid

Afraid I will never learn
From what I've done in the past
The same errors will follow
For the die has been cast

A Day at Work

Open your eyes
That you might see
The world as I do
Isolated from me

Sitting in the dark
As people pass by
Claiming to be friends
But again they lie

No greeting exchanged
As they come my way
No nod – no smile
Nothing to say

Eight hours each day
When I catch their eye
Quickly turning their heads
I give a silent cry

Watching the people
As they come and go
Claiming to be friends
Their actions are not so

A Child's Dreamland

Have you ever been a fireman
Or wanted to be an athlete
Were you ever there in an earlier time
That place where your dreams would meet

Have you ever been on a cattle drive
Tall in the saddle during the drive
Rounding up your stray ideas
Bringing all the dreams to your side

Have you ever walked on the moon
Or flew a jet across a star-filled sky
Have you ever visited that special place
Where your dreams would never die

I've been there in a different time
As everyone has in the distant past
Where childhood dreams captured our hearts
Wonderful dreams that never seemed to last

The Working Man

When did they grow out of diapers
I asked my wife the other day
When you were busy at work
It happened while you were away

When you were occupied with work
They learned to ride that old bike
Where was I during those early years
You were busy traveling on life's turnpike

While you were out earning money
You missed their first day of school
You weren't there to help with homework
But they still mastered the slide-rule

While you worked over to buy new clothes
They entered their high school years
Where they matured in knowledge
When they needed you, you weren't there

After working your fingers to the bone
While you were taking one of your naps
You missed seeing them graduate
You didn't even see they throw their caps

Now that they have grown and moved on
What good has all your hard work done
You provided all the necessities of life
But missed out on your daughter and sons

The Family Tree

In the forest of our life
There is a tree that stands out
Many have climbed its branches
Yet it is healthy and stout

Firm are its branches
Steady are the roots
One generation to the next
It is always bearing fruit

Established as the family tree
Firmly planted – centuries gone by
Many children have been raised
Many patriarchs have died

These lifelines of the past
And sacrifices that were made
Have all played a part
The foundation that was laid

From the love of a man
And the love of his wife
We gather here today
To celebrate our life

We come together today
From different regions of our nation
This gathering of family and friends
Spanning many years and generations

Crazy

Crazy you are
Crazy am I
Crazy we be

Crazy in life
crazy in mind
Crazy in love

You are Crazy
I am Crazy
We be Crazy

Life is Crazy
Minds are Crazy
Love is Crazy

Without you in life
Crazy is the word
Crazy in my mind

There would be no you
There would be no me
That would be Crazy

I may be Crazy
I know I'm Crazy
I'm Crazy about you

Love You

Will I love you
When you arrive

Will I love you
Into the night

Will I love you
In warm embrace

Will I love you
In the morn

I will love you
When you come

I will love you
Beyond the eve

I will love you
With each embrace

I will love you
Each new day

I will love you
For......
I love you

Rose

A rose for you
I picked myself
Holding it out in Love

Come stoke the peddles
With your gentle touch
See how straight the stem

In the warmth
Of your hand
The bud blossoms

Of course there are thorns
Sharp as can be
So I can.......
Stick it to you

Frogs

Come sit with me
On the Lily pad of life
As we dangle our feet
In the pool of love

Cattails abound
They blossom and blow
Spreading our love to the wind
Falling and planting new seeds

The butterflies fly
Spanning their wing
Soaring our love
To the sky

I will sit here with you
In our home on the lake
While we dangle our feet
From our Lily pad of life

Lois (aka Angela Davis)

Snapshots of emotions
That your heart does expose
Sharp as thorns on a stem
Beneath the fragrance of a rose

I see the hidden sorrow
When I look into your eyes
Painful times from your past
The tears you never cry

The fatefulness of hearts
That others do display
their acts of injustice
The words that they say

I will tell you the truth
As seen from far above
You are a child of God
A precious one He loves

And when I look in your eyes
I don't see as they do
Please don't judge me
From the actions of a few

Christmas Memories

Memories of the past
Reminiscent the times gone by
Remembering dreams we had
Seeing through our children's eyes

With the chill in the air
And the warmth in my heart
I know this is a time
That will never part

Distant mountains capped with snow
As frosties line the way
Snowflakes dot the sky
As children are at play

Little ones scurry about
On this Christmas day eve
Milk and cookies for Santa
For they still believe

They believe in a dream
A wonderland in their mind
Skating across the lake
If they are so inclined

Cheer spreads across the land
As a Santa rings a bell
Standing in a storefront
Merry Christmas he yells

Gifts are firmly tucked
Under the decorated tree
Wrapped in Christmas colors
One for you and one for me

With the ornaments on the tree
And the stockings hung so well
The children will gather about
As they all sing jingle bells

When the songs are over
And it's time for bed
Remind them once again
Of what God has said

This day His son was born
For all the world to see
That he is our Savior
And only He can set us free

I Remember

I remember a time
Not so long ago
Dancing in our youth
With children in tow

I remember a time
Not knowing what we had
You were the mommy
And I was the Dad

I remember a time
Dancing in our youth
With children in tow
Blinded to the truth

I remember a time
They grew up so fast
I remember a time
Wishing it would last

I remember a time
They left in a hurry
I remember a time
When I used to worry

I remember a time
Words they used to say
I remember a time
That time was yesterday

Spilled Drinks

At the end of the day
As you walk in the door
The sound of little feet
Running across the floor

They tackle your legs
With eyes opened wide
Come sit with me daddy
I want to be by your side

So precious are the children
We raised in our youth
Little bodies of innocence
If only we knew the truth

After a long day of work
At dinner they spill their drink
Lashing out in bottled frustration
Reacting without even a blink

Their little spirits crushed beneath
The weight of our stress-filled day
Not thinking before we speak
Not knowing of the damage we say

All from a drink that is spilled
Causing them in their chairs to shrink
From the worries we have in life
We never stop to think

In the grand scheme of things to come
Life is full of drinks they will spill
If we just stop and think
They are still precious and fragile

These are my Thoughts & Ideas

Love is a dreamland
Meant only for dreamers
I should know
I once played there

Life is a circus
It keeps us entertained

Life is full of dreams
With the nightmare of realizing
They will never come to be

❄ ❄ ❄

Darkness

I don't like the darkness
Still
And desolate
A jail
No bars holding you back
Only the mental bars
Of your mind
Which are stronger
Than any metal

Movement

It doesn't move me so I can't write.
It's not a movement from here to there
but rather a movement from there to here.
If an object doesn't speak to me
or come across in such a way that it arouses my emotion
then I cannot write.
It has to speak to me on an emotional level
before I can function.

❄ ❄ ❄

Me

Don't ask me to be someone I'm not.
I have enough trouble just being me.

Accept me for who I am
And not that which you
Want me to be

❄ ❄ ❄

Life

Life
Suspended in confusion
Swaying back and forth
Bouncing off empty stars
Voyagers of loneliness
Hollow Gutless spheres
Destine to survive
Living out their remaining lives
IN solitude

❄ ❄ ❄

She's just a burned out tube
In the back of my mind

❄ ❄ ❄

A forced thought on paper
A speedy reaction
A verbal response to vision
My method of writing
Effective for me

❄ ❄ ❄

Made in the USA
Las Vegas, NV
21 October 2022